Inflorescence

INFLORESCENCE
SARAH HANNAH

T|P

TUPELO PRESS

First paperback edition September 2007

Library of Congress Control Number: 2007927237

Tupelo Press, Inc.

PO Box 539, Dorset, Vermont 05251

802.366.8185

tupelopress.org

Cover and text designed by William Kuch, WK Graphic Design

Cover painting, "Garden" by Renee Rothbein (1924-2001),

private collection; used by permission

Tupelo Press is an award-winning independent literary press that publishes fine fiction, non-fiction and poetry in books that are as much a joy to hold as they are to read.

Tupelo Press is a registered 501(c)3 non-profit organization and relies on donations to carry out its mission of publishing extraordinary work that may be outside the realm of the large commercial publisher.

Inflorescence. From Latin, *in* + *florescere* to begin to bloom. **1**. a (1): the mode of development and arrangement of flowers on an axis (2): a floral axis with its appendages; *also:* a flower cluster. **2**. the budding and unfolding of blossoms: FLOWERING.

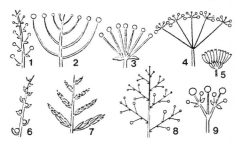

inflorescence 1a(1): *1* raceme, *2* corymb, *3* umbel, *4* compound umbel, *5* capitulum, *6* spike, *7* compound spike, *8* panicle, *9* cyme

Acknowledgments

The author gratefully acknowledges the following journals in which the poems in this volume have appeared or are forthcoming, some in slightly different form:

AGNI: "Alembic"
American Literary Review: "Winged Euonymous"
Bellevue Literary Review: "Night Nurse"
The Fairy Tale Review: "Diana, Hunting Words," "Flights below Waking," "Fair Seed-time," "Progressive Dreaming"
Gulf Coast: "Read the House"
The Harvard Review: "Sky Pencil," "The Riddle of the Sphinx Moth"
Ibbetson Street: "A Daughter Proposes Lithium," "The Haunted Suburb"
Interim: "Dried Flowers"
The National Poetry Review: "At Last, Fire Seen As a Psychotic Break," "The Leaded Windows," "Eternity, That Dumbwaiter"
New Millennium Writing: "Yes, Fiddlehead Ferns Are Even Older Than the Anglo Saxon Form"
Parthenon West Review: "Twinflower," "Tread-softly," "Inflorescence"
Painted Bride Quarterly: "The Safe House"
Poetry Review (London): "Blessed Thistle," "The Missing Ingredient"
Rattapallax: "True Forget-me-not," "Rue D'Aiguillon"
Southern Humanities Review: "Earliest Memory"
The Southern Review: "Haruspicy," "Azarel," "An Elegy for Bells"
Sou'wester: "The Garden As She Left It"
"Northampton, Massachusetts" was reprinted in *Chance of a Ghost: An Anthology of Ghost Poems,* ed. by Philip Miller and Gloria Vando, 2005.
"Night Nurse" was reprinted in *The American Journal of Nursing, 2007.*
"At Last, Fire Seen As a Psychotic Break" appeared as poem of the day on VerseDaily.com, October 16, 2006.

Special innumerable thanks to, first, the women who tended her—Pat, Jendih, Monica, Sylv. Those without whom this manuscript would not exist: Jeffrey, who made it true & changed my life, and Margaret, for all she does & who she is. To my dear friends & guiding forces: Zarina, Cynthia, Randi, Suzanne, Kate, Eva, Kathy Eden, Ted Tayler, Milton, and Marshall; for invaluable guidance on the manuscript: Martin Mitchell, Richard Wollman, Stephen Massimilla, Chris Tanseer; and thanks to the Virginia Center for the Creative Arts, where this book was begun and finished, and to those persons who happened there at that particular point in time, Summer 2006. Y'all know who you are. Finally, to my family: my father, Harriet, and Jessica, with love.

For my mother, Renee Rothbein (1924-2001)

———————

There is no death in mortal things, and no end in ruinous death. There is only the mingling and interchange of parts, and it is this that we call "nature."

—Empedocles

Where is the summer, the unimaginable,
Zero summer?

—T. S. Eliot

Contents

I
In Hospital

The Garden As She Left It

Locked, strung
With pollens, stirred by bees.
The cicadas burn

Their fine blue current.
At the center, two paths cross:
A ring of impatiens.

Their white petals lift to the air.
Are they waiting for the next departure—
Scrub jay, sulfur moth, the summer?

The paths lead outward
To a brick border,
A perfect circle squared.

On the gray wall of the house
A thin broom slants,
The air around it furious.

The dim figure of the woman,
The recent flutter of hands.

Common Creeping Thyme (Serpillum à serpendo)

If only it were just a lousy herb
That issued feeble tendrils slowly, now and then
Relinquishing some tiny blooms, its basest

Essence known to all (good on chicken).
Not a chance. Time tricks and trumps us, ropes us
In; floods and won't be stanched; speeds

Like this anarchic ER's rolling cots that bump
And skate all up and down the too-bright halls,
While you lie in a corner weeping dactyls (AH ha ha)

Until I reach you, grab your hands. If love's
Time's fool, I'm full-on shmuck, lured rushing back
Two state lines on a crappy bus for yet

Another of your episodes: an overdose
Borderline lethal, perhaps; a minor
Conflagration on the kitchen counter;

And now: an alleged inability to write checks,
Dial numbers. A Neuro intern appears,
Leans cotside, condescends to cross

Examine you on dates and names until
You shout at me Get RID of him! But him's
A her, and I admit I've never seen you

Quite like this before. We wait and curse
While aides placate us with stale crackers
And CranGrape juice. I decide to make

You name me every herb you grow so expertly
In pots behind your place. *Parse,* you offer first;
A man approaches, wagging films. He's terse.

"Shadow—Lung: Pneumonia." *What? Sage,* you grin;
Another page dispatched post-haste, younger

Than the first. He's clutching your CT:
"Tumors—left brain, three." And then a third,
Too young to grow a beard, steps forth, sucks in

His baby's breath, annunciates: "Metasta—"
Rosemary! you holler, *Rosemary!* as your arthritic hand
Smacks down in triumph on the piled white sheets—

"Sized," he concludes, then speaks slowly to my face.
"It doesn't look good." I turn to you, repeat
The clause. You beam. You've always wanted

A brain tumor, some definitive (read: physical)
Disease people will breathe above a whisper,
Some Bette Davis blight that brings Claude Rains

To your side, or better, your ex-husband from
His wife, and I'd go along with you laughing,
Waving *Hi!* to all who scurry past;

Laughing, god, so strangely laughing, but now
I know a shape of Time I've only seen
You paint—trumpet, bone, and wing, and I pray

To the fluorescent ceiling: Stay this Creep;
Shut this book right now, I'll read it later;
Let's fly back inside another spring

When I am low, just at your hem, knowing
Only that woods don't end and sun
Patters into shade, and we run down

Narrow paths to look for fern and toad
And early flower.

Yes, Fiddlehead Ferns Are Even Older
Than the Anglo Saxon Form

They thumb,   determined through

Moss, mushroom   mile of loam

Displacing rock   and rhizome.

Look! Look!   you shout, your lithe

Finger pointing   past purple

Crocus, which now   seems common, quaint,

Next to these naked   hairy nubs,

And since you burn   so overmuch

In ecstasy,   I see:

Stands of them   spiraling, white

In the silent wood;   symphonies,

As invisible fingers   fret along their necks,

And bows weave   under boughs.

And I will that   I will not forget them,

Though we may,   you and I, turn

Away, quite often,   apart (two stalks

Scrolling off,

I'll remember how

Just as, after

You call my name,

Beside yourself,

As if no one or

Been born to anyone

not speaking);

you called to me,

any absence,

should I appear—

a burst of joy

nothing had ever

or anything before.

Diana, Hunting Words

Seems like she just keeps running through her woods,
Grasping at violets, brambles, burrs, stumped utterly.
Nouns, those faithful slender hounds, those

Tender lagomorphs, have turned
On her and flown, soft haunches gone to flexion,
Swifted deep into a burrow.

Is it some kind of infection, all this spit
And struggle? Her brow's a furrow.
She parses grasses, lifts her arrow, points, can't see.

Don't ask her what she wants for lunch;
She'll just start hunting *turkey*, gesticulating
Chicken salad, tuna fish, but no such utterances

Come; they've swelled and stuck inside her brain
And dally in a florid meadow, flirting
With her nymphs—all those *things,*

Those fucking things, you know!
Rabbit, rabbit; cigarette; taxi out of here;
Cigarette, *damn it;* nightgown; oncologist; rabbi;

And that other one, a pronouncement
Set as cement, a blight too large to voice,
Waits silently, inscribed in numbers on a chart

Clamped against a metal board, and it pours suddenly,
But there's no longer any word for rain,
Only cloud.

Haruspicy

In good old Greece, to read futures in entrails,
The scatter of bird bones and guts on a beach.
All day they shuttled you from floor to floor
Through narrows—CAT scan, X ray, MRI—
And then some canisters of chalky, endless
Barium you had to drink for lunch.
And then the murmur of the last contraption,
The room quite cold, below ground.
It doesn't look good, quoth the white-coated seer.
But the bone scan—stars and hails fixing,
Falling through black sky, or drifting in a sea,
Inching forward with the tide,
Approaching us as if we were a shore.
We watched and watched the screen after the test
Was through. *Oh yes!* you almost shouted,
Neither one of us entirely surprised.

Macbeth's Problem

You never think it's really going to happen—
That Burnam wood will come marching
Down to Dunsinane—

Until, suddenly, your wife's got OCD,
And babies visit you in dreams,
Clutching eucalyptus.

And then those trees start walking,
I mean downright trouncing, toward you.
They do not come in peace,

And they're not willows or any other
Delicate variety; they're rowans,
Oaks, and ash,

And they will kick your ass to Cardiff.
Hello? You were so damn hot and ready
To jump the life to come,

You misread all the signs, and now it's Act V,
And you can't rinse out what you've done,
Can't redeem the time

Like Prince Hal, and besides, this one's a tragedy
Well into hour two; the place is packed with folks
Who've paid good money

To watch you go down bloody with a bough.

Azarel (Angel of Death)

Literally translated from the Hebrew, the word means *helps God.*

Death the lawyer adjudicates between us.
We can't stray too far, can't kill each other,
for Death, the honorable, presides; superior
Court judge Death comes down
And we settle, or else he settles us,
The endless squabbles and rejoinders,
Dust-ups, slanders, torts,
Described in dockets, assigned ten-digit numbers;
Death tries, he hears both sides, his clerk
Transcribes in shorthand but it all comes out
In tomes—CT—computerized tomography.

Death the social worker wears dark sunglasses,
Wide and square, advocates for only children,
Frequents terms like "push your buttons,"
Takes off her hat to my endeavors, gives
Audience on benches out of earshot
Of your room.

Death the hospice nurse dons tie-dyed shifts,
Dreams of fried plantains, and recommends a mist
Of baby oil in water, frozen grapes for hot days.
You want to slap her sometimes
When she gets excited about baths, as if a bath
Could help you, *Cut the new age crap, Death,*
You want to say, give me the pill, the triple dose;
Call in the order.

Call him in by any name:
Death swift or death fleet-footed,
Stalwart soldier, guarantor,

Executrix, executioner, panderer, pan-handler;
Death the cicatrix,

Death the figure.
You honored him in portraiture—
A winged thing with narrow hands and trumpet,
A butterfly of bone. You memorized
His scaffolding, held his sweet
Firm head and expostulated

As Faust or Hamlet did.

Death the lover.
You loved him many years.
Willed your body over, will after will
To his dominion, like Juliet you called him
From your sill, *wherefore,*
But just before the bell could ring
You always double-locked the door.
You teased him, courted and seduced him;
Whored him, married and divorced him;
Coaxed, cuckolded, and cozened him;
You high-stakes rolled, you bet the house
And won, but now, my dear,
He's really come.

II
In the Old House

Alembic

Still, a ruthless contraption.
You cannot work it backwards.
A trace, anemic limb within a sprawling wood,
A random pool of silt through a funnel.
It's not alchemy, it's not miracle.
It's criticism. Winnowing.
From three hundred thousand spawn, five minnows.
That one brilliant salmon who flew out of the stream.
You lived somewhere for many days.
What can you retrieve?

High windows, white, with mullions,
The waving tops of aspen trees.

You lived somewhere for very long.
But the avenues by which you could recall it
Have been closed for new construction.
At some point your mind chose a few for you,
A lucky few among the millions.
It was a process, then process turned to dogma,
As cars in thick snow
Will do well to drive in tracks of other cars.
The same few pictures stand, and then again;
You rescue four, then three, then two.
High windows, the waving tops of aspen trees.

There's no way to reverse the still,
No way to widen the path.
The silt in the cup won't revert to its primary
Ingredients. You can't save even half.
Windows, the very tops of trees.
Perhaps a scrap of linen curtain also.

But not the slab of wood marked "Birds Only"
By the field, the inexplicably sawed-in-half Bud Light cans
Strewn along the road, some pale wildflower,
The long grasshopper genuflecting at your door,
And, least of all, how and when
Wind turned the iron arrow.

Panes, trees—

There had to be a house!

A house to hold the windows

(Worms threading through the seams),
And trunks to hold the trees (of an ilk
Your mind has since discarded),
And by the trees some kind of weather,
Never still,
Like the wasps that flung themselves against the panes,
And all the moving, unpinnable rest,
The terrible rest you don't name.

Flights below Waking

It is 1959.
My mother lives with my father;
She is painting in reds:

A study of a crucifix from St. Mary's Church.
I am not born;
I am light of foot and skipping

Down the western end of Beacon Street
In a dress—lavender blue, from the ballad.
I pass the even lawns,

The box hedges, each stone house
Broods in its draperies,
The windows dark, reflecting.

I turn up the drive to the school yard.
Moonlight winks off the metal slide;
Seven iron steps are ringing.

I rise, no wind
At my hem, and when the town
Is laid out below me I know

That I have stolen into a brilliant still life—
A decade—glinting, untroubled.
What else do I see?

At this height I can't be certain.
The air is thin, and all I hear
Is the click of the sign box

Where three roads connect,
And the yellow lights blink
Top to bottom: on-off-on-on,

Rhythmic warnings,
The crossing of children.

Fair Seed-time

Fair seed-time had my soul, and I grew up
Fostered alike by beauty and by fear.
—Wordsworth

A pregnant woman can't afford to laugh off
Superstition. April, she pads along the river,
Startled by the sudden pronouncements
Of crocuses, a hand of them lighting all at once.

She thinks the pheasant notices and is spooked
By it also. May, in fright, she runs home one afternoon
When Indian Pipe appears in her way—a single
Fleshy growth among the dark pine needles.

She hangs red around the nursery—cloths
And yarns, a pompon on the crib—Jewish charms
To ward off evil. She paints in brighter colors:
Tidal pools, a series, but she's careful not to stand

Too many hours. June: certificate of live birth
At eight p.m.: WITNESS MY HAND
AND THE SEAL OF THE CITY REGISTRAR.
After digits, limbs, and breath are all accounted for,

The notary will make several typographical errors:
The child's name will lose all *h*s; he'll ask the mother's
Occupation, and when she tells him *artist*
He'll type *housewife*. A side effect of labor will occur:

The skin beneath her thumbs will flush
And mottle, deep red—
A permanent crimson at the palms.

Earliest Memory

Still cribbed, in the gable
With the tall hemlock

At the window, in the lull
Of late afternoon:

Three crackles; the story
Record ended. I somehow

Climbed over the bars
And crawled down the hall

Along the narrow balcony
Over the stairs: the twisted

Iron railings on my left,
On my right, the cool white

Stucco wall. To the next room:
My mother asleep on the bedspread

Of dark maroon and brown.
Sunlight hung in the curtains.

I watched her lying there.
I already knew not to wake her.

Read the House

You try to read it in the windows:
The mood of the house.
You count the panes,
The silent ivy movements.
When the lights are out
The glass looks like water.

Inside, a floorboard creaks;
It chimes in like a clock
Even when no one crosses.
Some nights all the lamps are lighted,
The oriental carpet glows,
A record plays on the stereo.

The house welcomes you then.
But on the night you return very late
There's no mistaking it.
The house is shut, pitch-blackened,
The screen door locked from inside.

You will have to rip a hole
In the wire mesh, reach through the barbs,
And unlatch it. While you were out,
There burned a small, protesting fire—
A token pile of matches
And grocery lists in the kitchen.

Do not go in.
You have trawled across strange floors
And found pleasure;
You have found your own house lacking.
Wait on the edge of the lawn—
The hedges are neutral.

Wait until the windows are blue with morning,
And daylight comes
With all its indications.

The house does not forgive you.

At Last, Fire Seen As a Psychotic Break

It begins in the crux of beam and insulation,
Behind the sepia portraits of ancestors
On the bedroom wall. A wire burns through
Its cloth sleeve, overwhelmed
By the demands of modern current.

It splits into two antennae,
Two probes in close space.
A spark shoots and sows in a post,
Then it starts to race—
Hungry, reckless,

Through the dry skeleton of the house.
Go to the wall. Can you see it?
Every episode is different.
Will it burn a seam or hole
To reach the open air?

You have to evacuate the family, but no one
Wants to go. And when they are dead,
And you are contemplating
The sticks, the wheezing ashes,
The iron pots melted to pools on the lawn,

The authorities will say it was structural.
Now that you think of it,
There were warning signs, gestures:
A flaming toaster,
A persistent aggressiveness.

On the littered ground in hindsight
You devise solutions.

What if you'd paid it more attention,
Sworn off sleep, made tea—
Could you have quelled it?

What if you'd stood nightly by the wall,
Felt around for the heat,
Drawn a cold, wet cloth across the surface,
And, speaking soft words,
Held it?

Westwood Lodge, 1980–1990

And then again, you go west, to that perennial
Resort at the end of the bending street, row of pines,
Where Sexton strolled through noon, made mocassins,
And danced in a circle: the Summer Hotel.

Why every tumid season, cicadas burning blue,
Beetles mounting one another, chewing all the flowers,
Do your pupils pinpoint, does your breath sour?
I call the police, who've nothing else to do

("Safest city in America" or so our town's ordained);
They arrive in flashing squadrons: at least eleven
Armed, sturdy men, five cars, for one uneven,
Overly-sedated woman past sixty. You've downed

Some sedatives with wine. How many? Your swoon
Gives none away; the Xanax bottle lies beneath the bed
With cigarettes and nylon socklets, so your stomach's pumped
Just in case. You always make it known to someone

Swiftly after it's been done: you will be saved. Inside,
Double-locked, you wait in line to use the phone. (Twenty-five
Years later, I still dream you're calling; you're alive,
Away someplace, but a vast conspiracy of bureaucrats hides

You from me. I wake, cried out. Does it mean, and where?)
Back then you reached me, asked for cigarettes,
Stockings, underwear, and the small two-volume set
Of Redon (ed. Rosaline Bacou). It doesn't matter

That the text's in French—it's got color plates.
While you're gone, I have the house to myself,

Turn the radio up, sing to the bookshelves,
Across the stucco arches, to the ceiling's walnut

Beams: Jay and the Americans' "This Magic Moment,"
With some irony, but not quite so much
As one might think, considering the lawn's gone thatch,
Burned brown, you're in lock up, and my paycheck's spent.

Speaking of lawns, ours was once all sun and dapple.
Childhood. A man mowed, a woman watered.
Something had to rot, go sour; someone ate the apple.
God died in the yard, à la Søren Kierkegaard—

In the doom of the downward slash: Existentialism
One-Oh-One, for frosh. I lie out and rub
Baby oil on my legs, hope to burn. God's a white grub.
He ate the lawn, but we can't afford to exterminate him.

Upside: you can't yell at me for wasting time lying
In the sun *(to please a man?)*. Downside: the docs
Tell me each time you come back in, they'll lock
You up for longer. If this crazy summer torquing

Doesn't stop, they'll put you somewhere else
For good (when we've run through the insurance)—
An institution of the state. No moondance,
Cakewalk. Or maybe dancing all the time in circles.

But for now, the asylum grass we walk on's trimmed,
Thick, and green. We watch the sky from Adirondack
Chairs. I bring flowers—cosmos, phlox, and hollyhock,
Your favorite—from our garden. Then, on a whim

One day, I arrive early, to your delight; I'm the only one,
After all, who comes. I've packed your acid-free
Paper and watercolors, though you didn't ask. *Forgive me,*
You say, *I'll paint planets.* Best thing I could have done.

A Daughter Proposes Lithium

The records of your rise and collapse
Are all over this place—

In the crags, the squall of gulls,
The scars on the salt-bitten tree.

If I could I would build you a wall,
Silver-white and glinting,

A shoulder for the break tide,
Like the Hindu who drapes himself

In stones for remedy.
The tree is low and gnarled.

Some days it seems staid;
Some days it terrifies.

Still, the birds
Look to it for landing.

Dried Flowers

After a long time alone
Your house fills with dried flowers.
You begin the collection in baking tins:

Yarrow, frostweed, red chokeberry,
Until, emboldened by your success
And by the growing absence

Of phone calls and visitors, you set them tumbling
From straw baskets on the floor, in bunches
On the tables and hutches, gilding

The old photographs, conversing
In spirals, some Byzantine logic
Elaborated long ago, conserved and replayed

And replayed in your mind. Similarly you come
To prefer the Victorian fadings of hydrangea
To the gloss and mettle of new leaf.

Pale roses claw around the banisters,
Colors drained to thin lines at the petals' edge,
The cell walls collapsed,

The skins gray and scarious.
They don't clamor for light or water;
They don't grow in strange directions.

In the dense air, they shatter, fine clouds
Of no color—your children—how they rise!
Without blame or complaint.

The Leaded Windows

There is a backward world
Figured in the coldest stare
Of staring through the pane
Some winter night when heat
From the old house scarces
Through cracks in time
Where wood has parted
Wood to breathe;
Keeping still, you might
See—not through to road—
But in to element: lead
And glass as they once were,
Boiling preludes to shape,
Precluding nothing—cistern,
Maelstrom, steam, the fluid past,
Still leaching in the wild blur
Of lead to glass along the frame's
Unquiet edge, exquisite storm
You can't penetrate, before
Event cures into artifact,
And sees becomes expects.
The lead (stay there) distorts.

Winged Euonymous (*Euonymous alatus*)

Torn from *America's Garden Book* (Scribner's, 1965)
Is a single page she couldn't be bothered to copy;

Actually, it's quite possible that on that day
She couldn't bear to go out her front door,

So she ripped out number 254, "Eastern Burning
Bush," underlined one phrase in red ballpoint pen,

Posted it my way: "the leaves are small
And finely toothed and in the autumn they turn

A deep rose in color, *a most beautiful and unusual shade.*"
Ours had been a shrub turned tree; two twisting trunks

Brought the whole creation well past nine feet,
Crimson in autumn (I AM WHAT I AM), tapping

At my bedroom window, as if proffering leafed counsel
To the leaded casements ("Don't take it all so hard"), not knowing

What was to come—a most beautiful and unusual shade
Of a blaze, windows melded, the whole house razed,

And then the tree gone ghost, felled sometime by someone
After us, a most beautiful and unusual shade,

From the genus meaning *named well.* I had thought
That it was mine, but it wasn't. It has flown;

It is flying.

III
In Home Hospice

Tread-softly *(Cnidoscolus stimulosus)*

Hell, this is a field without end,
Wider than a gate, athrum with
Insect wing and squawk. I might as well

Go swim in flame, but I can't swim,
So I'll just walk: bramble, spike,
And blame, without a single quenching

Drop of dew. Not a field—a ravine—
I mean a raving: You. And I'm
On double shift: daughter, nurse,

In double oxymoron: *home hospice.*
Some have said it's not worth saving,
This tiny family of Spurge: we two.

The hooks go in, the rash is swift, and
There's no poultice, only spur and spurned.
Even the milk sap burns. I've the urge to turn

And quit, but there's simply no one else to do it;
No one could or would—tread softly, that is—
Open the hand, toss the shoes and step back in,
Knowing what I know.

Night Nurse

Don't talk to me of Paris;
I have duties.
Don't talk to me of loss;
I bury pills in applesauce.

Come dusk, I'm in;
I draw the shade, the velvet cloak,
The dark antique brocade
You bought on sale.

It tells tales—tall, elaborate—
Of fates and tulips, groves,
Garden gates. You look at me
And know it's late;

It's almost time. Still, this spate
Is ours: nocturne, tantrum,
Morphine sulfate,
Pudding, needle, nightie.

The other shift is tidy.
The one by day, in white,
Is a woman full of god,
Her hair commanded, cloth and curler.

Such effort signals optimism.
She hand washes your dresses to dry
In the sun. She sings and scrubs, reads scripture.
She never curses, not even when you hit her.

Night's your scourge, your lackey.
I can't be fired or expelled. Rather,

I can be fired many times and still
Return each twilight; ring your bell

At seven. And you look at me with dread;
You look at me with spite and think of ebbing,
The fugitive and late-to-bloom,
The hoary loom above the bed.

Put it away with the dust pan and broom
In the smeared closet.
Deny me, all my implements—
This bed of sharps, this wound clock ticking,

This chamber pot and sickroom.
Forget us, every one, tomorrow,
And slide the morning in
Like a fresh dose, a clean spoon.

Sister Morphine

Bustles in her dark body
In the army hospital;

In the Stones' saddest ballad;
On our highest kitchen shelf.

I keep her for you—
Cerulean, sublingual mixture

Clad in brown glass.
Flying nun, she soars

From syringe to vaulted chamber
Beneath your squirming tongue—

Angel of Mercy, Sister of Care,
Until all you can ask for is more.

Slow song in A minor, she releases
The tone-deaf choir in your chest, eases

The rattle and stricture,
And what's left of your lungs takes the air.

Sister, she slackens,
Though a drop of her spilled on the skin

Will pull it tight as a snail
Shot back in its shell,

In the sea's wake sound asleep,
Spiralling off somewhere.

Indian Pipe *(Monotropa uniflora)*

You rattle in the bed, and I think of that flower,
Countless crowded voices seeking egress
Through a single waxy byway.

What's that awful noise? you ask.
Technically, it goes by three nouns:
"Rales, crackles, crepitation." Nurse and booklet

Promised it would be this way, like
The sound of someone sucking on the final
Dregs of soda through a straw. But when you

Ask, I swear it's the bookshelf creaking
From humidity; two woodpeckers out of synch;
Three geese choking on crab grass;

Four red-faced men a-coughing
From the bleachers at Fenway; five cups of coffee
Brewing in the percolator. *Don't be funny,*

You manage to say. Okay—six renditions
Of some contemporary flute solo
(Opus 47 in d minor); seven mice scratching

Inside the walls of our old house;
Eight hours passing noon.
Once, you found it full grown suddenly

In pine needles by the river: one flower, with one turn,
Or so the Latin. It terrified you—the flesh-like color,
And the fact that there was only one. You ran home

And looked it up. Like so many things, it had
Three names, three aspects:
Indian Pipe, Corpse-plant, Ghost-flower;

Single; terminal; nodding.

Blessed Thistle *(Cnicus benedictus)*

Let's go ahead and bless these double crosses,
These leaves about to stick us in a hundred places;

It's purported to protect from evil, plague, and harm,
And, according to the Bard, "it is the only thing for a qualm."

"Get you some of this and lay it to your heart," while
I run around and say some kind of benediction, try to smile.

Or maybe I'll grind it, make an herbal tea called Mother's Milk
For sale, they say, in California, or simply tear apart a thorny stalk,

Run it through my hand, draw it cross my wrist,
And make some sign, above the bed, to hold you fast—

Some auspicious symbol made of English dross and blood
(To you, a dram of anything from England must be good)—

To scare away what makes you cry for help,
What makes you call out *Mum!* to keep

You a bit longer, breathing here with me.

Inflorescence

How can you, who dosed yourself
With death so many times, be terrified
Of dying? I try singing folk songs
To calm you: "Greensleeves,"
"Scarborough Fair"; I read our favorite
Song from *Cymbeline*—"Fear no more,"
But nothing stops the shouts: *Mum, help, Mum.*
Can you see her, your rotund English mother,
All brisket, chicken fat, and bustle, a sparkling
Ruby brooch pinned to her wide breast, slicing
Fried egg pancakes into soup in some ideal
Jewish kitchen somewhere above my head, or,
My lady, do you call to me?

We're worn through, paced out like this second-hand
Persian rug beneath the rented hospital bed
And commode (no longer any use). Your fists
Strike the sheets. There's nothing I can do.

All around us: flowers.
Costly exotics jetted post-haste from La Jolla,
Genetically mastered for astonishment
Through excess: Double Boulevardia,
Triple Gardenia, nursed in hothouses,
Delivered to the door in polystyrene boxes.
Kind of ridiculous, you said, when you could speak.

Canterbury Bells your former painting student
Drove down one day from Maine,
In a graceful vase of milky green. How we
Gasped over those, tolling, pale blue, color
Of the liquid morphine.

And the handpicked bunch my friend
Brought from her garden in Somerville,
Clutched in tin foil: Meadow Rue,
Celandine, waving in the air conditioner's
Tempered breeze. They won't last the week.

Mum?

I flip through Webster's Dictionary.
There are names for how they show themselves—
Patterns of arrangement.
Such things, I reckon, do not die. I read:
"Raceme, umbel, corymb, cyme."

You quiet, close your eyes.

Between the rattle and the oxygen machine:

"Spikelet, spadix, strobile."

After leaf and petal fall,
Up and down the graying bones,
The innate structure of the flowers.
You can see it when the finery is gone:
How their blooming plans itself:
Queen Anne—Compound umbel,
Exponential, known to sweep
Entire fields in lacy white, coup
After coup of radial symmetry.

Mum.

I can't tell you where you're going,
And I won't make up some story.

"Raceme, umbel, corymb, cyme"—

Mum, what's this?
I clasp your wrists.
Not now, just you and me, this room?
Corymb, cyme—capitulum?

True Forget-me-not *(Myosotis scorpioides)*

The complementarity of color
Is not hearsay, neither conjecture nor
Whimsy. It's true. You spoke it: yellow-blue,
Blue-yellow. *Look,* you said, *the beech and sky*
Blaze against each other on clear fall days.
Chicory burns in a field of yarrow.
One spectrum trembles on another, two
Primaries vie; it's too much fray—you start
Upright and stare at me with no eyes, eyes
Rolled back to white; they fix me, as the blood pools
In the small of your back, at your elbows.
Are you going walking by the river?
How violently you take your leave—blue petals,
Yellow lymph blooming up from the core.
Forget you? Truly, never.

IV
Inflorescence

Eternity, That Dumbwaiter

Still hauls through the house—
Not the house today,
Or twenty years ago, or more,

But the plain conception of the house,
Before toll of tread and deed—
The house before. Still pulls

Past eave and girder, hoar cordage sworn
Around an iron circle, rope of twisted rope
That rolls along the pulley

In the attic gable, through the cedar
Rafters, behind the sealed dormer window,
And all the ragged white ephemera

That happen to be flapping there.
Still flies with purpose, past
The inquisition of the shifting

Boards, past stucco, plaster,
Iron, lead—the ages—bronze
And silver, fieldstone, flame,

Age of sickness, age of pause.
And so it waits at ground
As four dour, burly men

Heave in the load. It buckles
With the box; it stalls; it will not go,
And then it rallies, then it's off—

Resumes its loop and chore,
Determined servant through the stories.
Someone's calling from another floor.

An Elegy for Bells

Do you remember the sound of the old phone ringing?
A real bell in it—the rotary phone
On the upright table
Between your mother's room and yours.
It had weight; it had recurrence—

Molecules shifting, sound propagating
Through the house, off the yellowed walls
And the iron railing. Do you remember
The ring and its aftermath, a quartertone
Higher? There are two sides to everything:

The ring and its ghost, the one
Calling and the one called.
With a strange gray receiver
At your chin you have called the house
And heard that ring—smaller,

But no less palpable; you have heard it ring
Some forty times and wondered
If she were dead or merely sleeping;
You have pictured her lying there
Letting it ring, now and then

Shouting back at it; you have pictured her there
On the edge of unconsciousness,
Gently stirred by the sound, chasing after it:
A trail of pale blue circles
In her thickening dream. You have stood

In your room, your one bag packed
(She has asked that you leave and not return)

And waited silently for it: from the next town,
The unlikely deliverance—
Your father, the police, or at least

The psychiatrist. You have ventured out
In the bald hall light only to find
A certain deadness, sometimes,
In the earpiece: the cord cut,
A crop of multicolored wires blooming

On the rug. You have taken tea in other houses,
Heard the ring, and declared it an annoyance;
After a few years of this it rang less often,
And today, in different rooms, in a lightweight
Flip-top shell, it barely rings at all;

Gone, the resonance,
The tick of modern digital tones
Completely formless, forgettable.
You miss the thunder.
There are two sides to everything:

The pain in it ringing,
And in it ringing no longer.

Northampton, Massachusetts

I wander tree to tree, an idle guest.
The names are stamped on metal plates
And nailed to the trunks: Sugar Maple,
Elm, Cedar-of-the-Lebanon.
It is autumn, Friday afternoon;
The walks are empty.
The elm is pure gold serrate,
The cedar a series of thickets.
I stand by the burning maple.
In the stillness, a ghost:
My mother running towards me
Across the lawn of broken leaves.
She is bringing me the reddest.

Rue d'Aiguillon, Quebec City

Fearful, having wandered off and found
Myself alone inside a narrow whitewashed alley

Of vendors and ancient scabbing stones
In Quebec City, I falter over commerce, falling prey

To false cognates: *Je voudrais exchanger*
When I mean *changer*. Blushing,

I correct myself, and despite the bungle
The vendor grins and offers me a string

Of translucent yellow shells, calls me *jolie fille,*
And for the moment I believe him,

Sun aslant, articulating volumes—
Fissures in the crumbling rock—envoi

Borne in error to a solitary place,
The dull glass absenting from my eyes,

The oil veil lifting from the world.

The Missing Ingredient

'Sixty-eight, I was two, Mariat harpsichorded "Love is Blue,"
Everything sunflowered, serene; my father swears "Even
Renee was happy then." Housewives read the *Rubiyaat of
Omar Kayyam* (I have her copy), donned loose paisley
Tunics—there she stands, true as Kodak, dark bookshelves
On her right (most legible title: *The Hinge of Fate*).
Neighbors (actual surname: Hamilton) grew carrots, piled bees
In boxes; we stood still before the swarms. Was it all rot? Surely
Not! I've stacks of proof, just not enough ease, not enough juice.

The Riddle of the Sphinx Moth

An enormous body kamikaze-dives
At me from behind the eaves of a summer
Shack: a sudden blow between the eyes,

A hybrid whirr—half bird, half bee—she hovers,
Helicopters to the grass, and sparks: Long-short-long,
Morse code in creature-speak for *Get you gone.*

I run inside. What was she? A pair of dragonflies
Combined to mate like biplanes in a blitz
Seem cordial in comparison to this—the eyes,

Two narrows, solid black, or should I say,
Twin Stygian pools of fixedness,
Her torso thick, a pattern throbbing in the fur,

And what was that prodding in front of her?
A stick, a thin proboscis, twice as long as she,
Insinuates itself in jimsonweed—

Sucks out all the juice. Twenty quiet minutes pass
Until I hear a rattle on the glass;
The window's shaken out of frame—she's in!

She fouls the bed—the whole room's a sty.
I should flee. I shudder in my chair instead.
She owns this house, not I.

A buzz and feint, and with a glare
She's out the door. She owns the house,
Not me. I've solved the riddle:

All skirmishes aren't fatal;
All metaphors don't fly.

Threepence, Great Britain, 1943

My thrupenny bit bears a flower on its back:
A three-stemmed thrift plant, *Allium porrum*. It's a lesson—
Thrift—that I must learn and learn darn quick.

It's one my mother, a child of the Great Depression,
(Big and little *d*) knew well. I'll save you all the trouble,
Provide the proper shelf: this one's a confession.

At nineteen, my mother's mum birthed a girl
In a row house (scullery, outside loo) in Stokie,
London, 19 Aden Grove. Great ivy grows there still.

Forward to a Jewish ghetto in Chicago, year of coin.
My mother nineteen; her mum went funny,
Locked up and electroshocked, chomped down

On a bit to save her tongue. On scholarship at U of C,
My mother quit to help her father run his jewelry store—
Kept accounts and inventory, demurred to customers. She

Was always good at sums, but they were poor;
In a cold water flat behind the shop, she shared a twin
cot and constant lice with her younger sister,

Although in studio photographs (sepia-tone,
Costly, rare) their hair's in perfect rag-curled locks.
I have some snapshots of her, age thirteen,

'37, the coin's first issue. Slender, bathing-suited, she kicks
Sand at Margate, on holiday with her mum's dad, *Zeydee*,
Who bounced her on his knee and tended hollyhocks.

Mother, although you smoked and drank to excess, tried
Twice to gas yourself, ran cars into trees, you kept clever,
Kept just enough eggs by forty-one for me. (I'll tie

This one up quickly, folks.) Skip to 1985: another
Broken summer when you sent me from the house,
Read too much Woolf, and walked into the river,

Walked right out again. You got it wrong; it was the Ouse,
Not the Charles. You forgot the stones as well.
I was nineteen, home from college. We kept the police

On their toes. They strapped you to a gurney and stuck you in a cell
Below ground, worst ward (D) in hospital. Meanwhile, although
I worked overtime (boss and me), I couldn't save. I was fertile,

Didn't want to be. Today, at forty, in divorce, I wonder how
I've less of all you kept so carefully in store: money,
Space, fecundity. Three-flowered thrift. I'll learn it now.

Jewelweed/Impatiens

The first: domestic, tamped in pots,
Unloaded into wheelbarrows, fitted tight in plastic trays.
Her foliage is sweet: leaf hearts; her petals symmetrical and flat.
She bides inside your gate, keeps low and still,
Faints easily from lack of drink and too much sun,
Though on occasion, after dark, she might
Dare light your way along the primrose path
Of you-know-what. Summer's end, her ribbed pods
Swell, implore you for release.
Best keep her locked and watered.

Her wild twin just won't be bartered,
Won't be packed in sixes, sold, dangled from a fence.
She grows tall and full of juice along the river, woods.
And those gem-like mouths—red and orange wrath,
And laughter—simply nod, refusing to take fright
At foxes, squall, or stomping deer. Alone
On no man's land, she procreates at will,
Or wills wind or quill to pop her. Silver paths
Crisscross her leaves; it's just a fancy maze
That leads back where you started. Touch her. Touch her nots.

Sky Pencil *(Ilex crenata)*

So we're of one mind that there are two names for
Every real thing—in Latin, *Genus, species*—
More, if we can count the common ones from lore.
Many impartial

Parties call this poem's title tree "Japanese
Holly," but you should know right now: we aren't here
At all concerned with neutrality. My step-
Mother and father

Bought it for me, to block barbed wire that divides
My "city yard" from a parking lot. The root-
Ball hole had to be large; my then husband dug,
Nourished it with dung,

Peat moss, and mulch, while I circled, muttering
"Sky Pencil." I'm still saying it, seemingly
Out of the blue, but with care: the "eye" of *sky*
Emphatic, but not

Nearly as protracted as that terminal
"Sill." When my father visits, I point, repeat
With glee, "*Sky Pencil.*" He laughs. "That's not the real
Name," he says. "Aphids,"

I reply. "It has aphids. They're killing it."
"How will you find a cure," he says, "when you don't
Know the real name?" My father's a classicist.
Rather, I should say

He's an artist who paints in the classical
Style: no composition or tone off balance,

No expression without order. His oeuvre:
Dolorous women

Clothed, thinking, a vase or a peach beside them,
Or, if he's feeling wild, both. Were the tree his,
He'd know the Latin name. Still, I retain an
Obstinate preference

For the nickname as if it were true, as if
Trees could bridge the awful space splitting ground from
Cloud and shell from star, and Wordsworth's heart might leap
If he beheld—which

Brings me to the flip side of that coin of my
Begetting, the woman who'd have loved that name,
Who painted, let's say, quite a bit differently,
Colors off spectrum,

Flowers, heads, eye sockets, and skulls, floating, so
Thick, my inheritance: a hundred cracking
Canvases, cadmium red to *mars black*. Sometimes
Someone finds something

Unsettling in a certain light. There were names
For all that too: Borderline, Bipolar, Mad;
Vengeful, tender; refusing mood stabilizing
Medicines—but who

Could help adoring that common moniker,
Itself a piece of whimsy, ridiculous,
Dark cleft leaves inscribing heaven with sheer will?
So, I call experts

Who of course know every name, and I commence
A cure, as she now and then glances down from
Her work—freed from quill, lead, reed, even pen—
Rendering true forms.

Progressive Dreaming

Midnight, and you're scaling the windows
By the mullions, the sills' elaborate scrolls.
        You pull into the old house like a skilled burglar.
You are, actually, different: you're in high boots, your posture
        Has improved, your hair is longer.
And with that simultaneous awareness of dream and waking life,
        You steal across the upstairs hall to the linen closet.
Once, it held not only towels
        But deep white drawers with wooden boats
And packets of black-and-white photographs
        ("Ansco All-Weather Film") yellowing with acids.
You pull one out: the house under previous owner:
        A stout woman in sables standing proudly
On the dry, sunny lawn, a Great Dane at her side—
        This particular print
Defaced by the palmate scratchings of a fountain pen
        (Your mother drew in hedges to see how they would look).
The closet walls are papered
        With antique fleur-de-lis, each flower padded, a tiny pillow
In the wall in a regular pattern.
        Delighted, you press them, climbing the drawers
To the dark ceiling,
        Until your fingers stop at a cold brass latch.
At its release a trap door falls open, and with an ease
        That comes only in dreams,
You hoist yourself into the bottom half of a gabled room.
        The air is sweet with cedar.
On your left is a steep, slatted staircase,
        On your right, a grove of enormous zinnias
Made of embroidery thread and fenced in with rickrack.
        Above them, a blue crepe dress hangs on a nail.
It is teeming with finches and pearls;
        When it moves you hear the faint sound of flapping.

It belonged to the sable-coated woman—
A Vanderwyck of Boston, long dead.
You know the dress will fit you but it cannot be removed,
Just as you know another floor awaits you
In the gable.
But you have to leave. The new owners will return;
You'll be arrested for breaking and entering.
Again, the awareness, passing swiftly overhead:
In waking life the house burned to the ground.
You cross the room to a small open window.
You can see the whole neighborhood.
The moon glows pink; the giant pines are made of mint.
You breathe it in. On the sill, burnt into the wood,
A line of careful script:
"You are nine hundred feet in the air."

Five Years Passed Exactly, but Who's Counting?

Should you stare at flowers for any length of time
You'll note the myriad, ingenious ways
They devise to make themselves known to you and bees—

Bees more importantly, of course; it's a matter
Of persistence, survival, and so, presentation must be various.
Similarly, the dead will wink at you or knock you on the head:

A sudden silent snowfall in New York City;
All the chicory in Virginia bursting into bloom;
A wristwatch stopping at eight p.m. precisely;

A brown moth flying blithely in the front door
And landing on her signature in the corner
Of the oil painting of Icarus. (How much more

Can one stand?) All of it's just play,
Of course—nods and jabs from them, as if you needed
A refresher on tautology: the dead are dead;
Flowers are pretty.

The Haunted Suburb

The land plowed by tractors
Is haunted by oaks, by the circling
Protests of sparrows unnested.

The brick in the yard by the fiddlehead fern
Is haunted by the toad
Who lived for many years

Beneath it. When he climbed out
One day and didn't return,
The brick cracked in half.

And the suburb is haunted by girls.
Of indeterminate shape
And accommodating color,

Swift in nylon jerseys.
Their questions are whorled in new leaf,
Their names transcribed in the pokeweed's

Purple ink. You heard it
In the neighboring yards; the children's
Shouts and rhyming games

Reminded you of yours,
Grown and gone, and you've
Gone also, and the suburb

Is haunted by you; the beige
Mansion is haunted by the cottage
That burned in its place, and you

And I we pace those long
Halls nightly. And the suburb
Is haunted by girls—they have

Never left it, really—
A swatch of skirt, a curled
Hair will catch on a branch

In the felling of the tree, and I
Am caught on the land and it haunts me,
And we are running through the briar.

The Safe House

You don't speak of it, not ever,
But you make sure it's always there:
That remote, delicious contingency, the hold,
The hideout at the end of the narrow, nameless
Lane with no light, the long back road
That twists and forks relentlessly, so that
Unless you know the way, you'll never find it.
Unless your mind happens to work that way,
In which case, not only do you know damn well
How to get there (could walk it blind), you simply
Can't survive without it. A real house (Wood
Frame, Cape), unclaimed in any county
Book of deeds, unmarked on any map,
Unrung by doorbell or by phone.
A space without a title.
Just stop. Just think about that for a second.

Furnished simply: in the first room, a couch,
Two matching lamps, a hotplate, and a well-
Stocked bar; beyond, the bedroom and adjoining
Bath, a closet full of scoop-necked, small
Waisted satin dresses, a corset, heeled sandals,
Stockings. You don't have to plan beyond that;
In fact, all you really need's the impetus
And means to get there, both of which
Involve a man—two at most—chosen
With great care, of course; so often
They go south, soprano, pull that sucker
Punch on you. But this time, this one's
A pro; he puts it all together, really comes
Through: job (how grand, the larceny!),
Signal, getaway. You just have to wait
For the single playing card (king of diamonds)

Cantankerous Author's Notes

Inflorescence. The author originally wished this book to have two titles: *Inflorescence, or, How to Know the Wildflowers,* based on the idea, put forth rather insistently throughout this volume, that there are two names for everything. However, her publisher warned her that such a title would be quite long and might cause problems. Please refer to her previous book, *Longing Distance* (Tupelo, 2004), for an adventure in the graphical representation of the space-time continuum vis à vis book titles.

"The Garden as She Left It": the landscape of the garden is one frequently found in English and French gardens and is often called a *parterre.* The circle within the square or vice versa is also the figure known as the *mandala,* Sanskrit for "magic circle." The "woman" designed it with both in mind.

"Common Creeping Thyme": This delightful name for the herb was obtained from *Gerard's Herball* (1599), a favorite reference book of Shakespeare's, or so say the editors of the Arden editions.

"Haruspicy": the title refers to the ancient practice of divining the future from bird entrails. The more common word "auspicious" comes from the same root.

"Alembic": the title refers to an apparatus used in distillation.

"Flights Below Waking": the "St. Mary's church" is meant to refer the reader, should he or she please, to the corner of Beacon and St. Mary's Streets, on the border of Brookline and Boston.

"Westwood Lodge": Although Renee Rothbein and Anne Sexton did not visit Westwood Lodge in the same decade, Sexton did refer to it in her poetry and letters as "the summer hotel." See "You, Doctor Martin," and "Music Swims Back to Me" in *To Bedlam and Part Way Back* (1959) and

Anne Sexton: a Self Portrait in Letters, ed. Linda Gray Sexton and Lois Ames (1977). Westwood Lodge is not, of course, nearly as famous as that other Boston-area sanitarium, McLean Hospital in Belmont. In fact the author would venture that, judging by comments made by both women, Westwood Lodge seems to possess a genuine mental hospital "inferiority complex" regarding McLean's.

"Winged Euonymous": "(I AM WHO I AM)"—if you don't know where this is from or who is saying it, you're in big trouble. Go ask Someone. Exodus.

"Blessed Thistle": the quotation is from *Much Ado About Nothing,* Act III, sc. iv, Margaret advising Beatrice.

"Inflorescence": the dictionary is *Webster's Collegiate,* Tenth edition (1999).

"The Missing Ingredient": what's missing is in the poem. Go look for it. With a nod to Rachel Wetzsteon, absolutely.

"Sky Pencil": thanks to A. E. Stallings and Eva Salzman for help with the Sapphics.

"First Singing Lesson Ever, at Forty": for Gilda Lyons and everyone at VCCA. Sometimes artists' colonies can uncannily resemble mental institutions. For the time, this author prefers the former.

"The Hutch": the quotations are from the opening of *Hamlet,* Act I, sc. 1.

Sarah Hannah, 1966-2007
By Rachel Wetzsteon

My dear friend Sarah Hannah—poet, teacher, critic and ALSC
member—took her own life on May 23 of this year, at the age of forty.
The daughter of two painters, she grew up outside Boston, attended
Wesleyan, played in a rock band, completed a doctorate on the modern
poetic sequence in 2005 at Columbia (where I was lucky enough
to meet her), moved back to Boston, and taught courses in writing
and literature at Emerson College. Her first book of poems, *Longing
Distance,* was published by Tupelo Press in 2004, and *Inflorescence* is
her second book.

That's her life story in a nutshell, but setting it to paper I'm saddened
anew by how "bounded," in a great Dane's words, it feels. Sarah was one
of the smartest, wittiest and kindest people I've ever known—check
out the "Guest Book" of her online Boston Globe obituary for heart-
wrenching and heartening testaments to all these traits and more—and
it's still unfathomable that we'll never again eat flaming cheese at the
Symposium Greek restaurant in Morningside Heights, trade favorite
lines of Renaissance poetry, dissect a Hitchcock movie in lunatic detail,
exchange horror stories of the shifting tides of Po Biz, or watch in wry
delight as her frenetic pug Bridgette runs circles around her altogether
calmer lizard, a bearded dragon named Lucille.

Sarah was also an absolutely extraordinary poet whose work I urge you
to track down at once. Her poems—like the person who wrote them
—are learned, passionate, funny, observant, and wise. She embraced
eclecticism rather than opting for one style, mode, or tone, and the
result is not a deafening cacophony but a rich polyphonic record of a
wonderfully complicated mind in action. Like all poets worth reading,
Sarah knew stuff: astronomy, botany, art history, weather. She could
write a mean sapphic stanza, as well as some of the finest contemporary
sonnets I've seen. But she could also be downright hilarious. I think one
of my favorite poems, "After the Long Chard Season," nicely illustrates
this effortless blend of comedy and erudition. One year Sarah decided

to join an organic food-delivery company, but when she opened the first box, expecting gleaming fruits and vegetables, she found instead a startling profusion of leafy green matter. The poem she wrote about the experience closes like this:

Who knew there were so many greens?
Chive grass, Boston lettuce pollard,
Elysian shade of parsley boughs.
It might just possibly be true
That all that was undone is through.
These are the salad days.
These are the salad days!

Here Sarah, grafting a domestic mishap onto a Shakespearean allusion, gives us a striking parable of hope, at once playful and prophetic. I can't think of a better illustration of Eliot's account of how a true poet "is constantly amalgamating new experience; the ordinary man's experience is chaotic, irregular, fragmentary. The latter falls in love, or reads Spinoza, and these two experiences have nothing to do with each other....in the mind of the poet these experiences are always forming new wholes."

In another poem, the beautiful "For the Fog Horn When There Is No Fog," she urges us to give thanks whenever we can, since we never know what new threat might be lurking:

    there might be fog
And even squall, and you'll have nothing

But remembrance, and you will have to learn
To be grateful.

Indeed, there might be fog. Sarah's loss is inconceivable. But I'm learning to be grateful for my memories of her, and for the fact that readers who never got to meet this marvelous person can at least look forward to discovering her marvelous poems.